MW01483210

RISE!

The TAO
Of The DIVA

REGINA BROWN

RISE ! The TAO Of The DIVA
IS PUBLISHED BY:

MICHELANGELO PUBLISHING
8491 WEST SUNSET BLVD. #160
LOS ANGELES, CA. 90069
Email: scijung@michelangelopublishing.com

www.michelangelopublishing.com

© copyright 2001 Regina Brown All Rights Reserved

Distribution
GREENLEAF BOOK GROUP
660 ELMWOOD POINT
AURORA, OHIO 44202
800-932-5420
www.greenleafbookgroup.com

Library of Congress Catalog Card number: 2001- 096845

ISBN: 0-9715152-0-4

This book in its entirety or any portion, may not be reproduced by any means, including but not limited to mechanical, electronic, audio, video, or photographic. Storage in a retrieval system for the purposes of transmission or for the purpose of copying, for public or for private use, either partially or entirely, is prohibited.

Fair use such as brief quotations embodied in articles and reviews are permitted. For permissions and reprint information, please contact the publisher.

The author and publishing company make no medical claims whatsoever. The contents of this book are strictly the opinions of the author and are offered for informational purposes only. No technique in this book is offered as a substitute for medical attention nor are they prescribed as treatment. The author and publishing company assume no liability or responsibility to any person(s) or entity with respect to any loss or damage caused directly or indirectly by the information contained in this book.

Photography: Mel Peters for Directions and Exposure
Art Design: Henry Castellanos
Web Design: Kevin Ferlin

First Edition Paper Imprint 2001
Printed in the United States of America

The pulse of repetition courses through the veins of this dissertation

To the skeptics...
It is a mere reverberation of an age old spewing,
that which has been foretold.

To those that doubt, I say,
The voice of the Most High bends sweetly to all ears

I hear His voice amidst the mountains of Yahweh
I see His face in the mirror of Mohammad
I seek His wisdom in the stillness of the Buddha
I revere His words in the Holy Scriptures
I can rest in the arms of His only begotten son, Jesus

Sound, Sound, Sound the bells...
And sound them again and again

Let no man run away from his true reflection
For his beauty is glorious

To the true Diva...

Rise!

This is the call to awaken the soul

It is the great force of the Mother River
Sprouting out to all of her tributaries

It is the Dare to flow freely

It is the beacon chisled from the sun to shed light upon the way.
Take from "Rise!" only that which speaks to your heart

Leave the rest to the wind
To those who wallow in mediocrity...

Let them moan!

For this is

The
TAO
Of
The
DIVA

At the core of every heart…
every wish that is whispered in silence
unfulfilled
every desire that dares to fly on clipped wings
casts an anchor upon a love swept sea.

Each one of us possesses the magic to embrace, empower, and immerse ourselves in the sweet euphoria of love. The secret is to intimately define it, live and breathe it, no matter what, and allow this beacon to shine as it calls forth into our lives its mirror reflection in others.

In order to receive love… we must be… love.

For some of us, it is a flickering flame of
a "love lost" in faded glory.

Boring!
Stop living in the past.

You rule!
It's a new day… Go down in history with your very own,
"Greatest Love Story Ever Told."

Are you ready to have it all?

Originally, I planned to write two books, "A DiVaz Guide to Life" and "Infinite Resolution, 9 Steps to Perfect Love." Each one offers a perspective on love and transformation, a plan for a commitment to excellence, and each book offers something that the other does not. However, they constantly overlapped. So I stopped fighting it and decided to "Go with the Flow."

What you see is what I give you from my heart...
    the part of me,
        Rising out of life lessons,
            painted in great joy and pain,
                but lessons none the less.

I have written this book to find myself...
To remind myself that what my life has given me
            places me here, on this path.

The Outcome is incidental for that is Destiny.
No one can design their stars...
        but dreams do come true
          and

Miracles
      belong to anyone that dares
           to call them into being.

The Bottom line

What are you made of ?

Who are you when you look into the mirror of life

and you see the "Real you" staring back?

Do

You

Like

What

You

See

?

What is a DiVa?

A DiVa is someone that Rises to the unimaginable

and

becomes

the

Star of her universe

She is a relentless warrior that will stop at nothing short of victory.

She is gracious

graceful

intelligent

patient

compassionate

respected

loving

and

Fabulous!

Are you a DiVa ?

The Tao of The DiVa is a journey of transformation.

We will peel away all of the layers of the past

and magically evolve into "Goddesses."

We will laugh, maybe even cry a little.

Best of all,

we will come together in the

Realization of the Self,

A fabulous, flawless, wonderful

You

who just happens to be a DiVa !

RISE

The TAO Of The DIVA

RISE! The TAO Of The DIVA

Table of Contents

What is love ?

Love exists only in present tense
As each moment in time dawns anew
Love recreates itself... increasing its momentum

Love travels faster than the speed of light
Its Divine emanation illuminates the Sun within us
Love is sacred and pure
It is Life Force
It encompasses all... yet holds on to "No Thing"

It is Bliss
It is Attainment
It is Samadhi

Love bursts forth like Spring's first opening of a rose
It releases a fragrance intoxicating all that inhale it
It is powerful... yet never forced
It is delicate... yet it is fortified with integrity
Love is Giving... Giving is Love

Love exists only in present tense
As each moment in time dawns anew
Love recreates itself... increasing its momentum

Love travels faster than the speed of light
Its Divine emanation illuminates the Sun within us
Love is sacred and pure
It is Life Force
It encompasses all... yet holds on to "No Thing"

It is Bliss
It is Attainment
It is Samadhi

Love bursts forth like Spring's first opening of a rose
It releases a fragrance intoxicating all that inhale it
It is powerful... yet never forced
It is delicate... yet it is fortified with integrity
Love is Giving... Giving is Love

囍

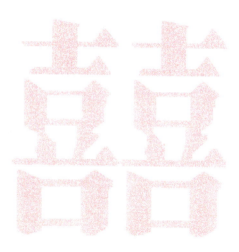

The Divaz 10 Commandments

Creating a New You...

1

If your heart says "NO"...

Let it go!

Don't allow any person, place or thing to stay in your life
if it breeds negativity.

Time is our greatest teacher for it reveals all. In order to truly become a *DiVa*, you must first know yourself. I consider the life process a cosmic game. Picture yourself as Dorothy on her way to Oz or Cinderella trying to get to the ball. Two *DiVaz* on the path that would change their lives forever. They were both looking for love. They were both looking for Home.

Home is the place where we feel the greatest sense of security. Home resonates the strongest energy of love. (Not everyone vibrates to this energy.)

Many of us view our lives as hopeless, dead-end streets. We are oftentimes complacent and willing to accept the hand dealt to us, even if we are miserable and our intuition tells us that we deserve better.

If you find yourself in a place where nothing feels right, consider yourself lucky. That is the DiVaz "barometer for change." It is your "Divine Right" to redesign anything and everything that does not make you absolutely ecstatic. I can hear someone saying, "There is no such thing."

When you design your life, you get to pick the fabrics, the patterns, and the colors that make you happy. You are not required to hang on to negative energy. The people, places, things, even relatives that are all negative "isms," **All Go Buh Bye!**

When we remove from our lives that which does not serve our highest good, we get to know ourselves. Think of it as Spring-cleaning.

We become okay with the **"Me"** alone time that most people dread. When you can be happy with yourself, your heart speaks to you. This is the time your intuition begins to divulge the DiVaz renewal plan.

DiVaz don't use phrases that begin with

Would of, Should of, Could of....

DiVaz live in the "Now."
The magic of the present tense fills each page of our lives with adventure and majesty. When it comes to matters of the heart, the same theory applies. Negative energy is a beacon that signals the need for change.

Change is a DiVaz new best friend.

When it is over.

It's over.

DiVaz do not dare look back.

It is extremely tasteless!

Don't be a Drama queen and wallow in the "Woe iz me, I luv-ded him," vibe. (Yes, the spelling is correct.) That's what you sound like when you are having a Trauma Queen moment, emotionally inarticulate!

I want you to try this. Each day when you wake up in the morning, take time to give thanks to the Supreme. Reflect on the Miracles of the day before. When you consciously identify even the smallest blessing, your faith increases.

You begin to see that you won't ever be forgotten. You see the Divine plan that is uniquely yours in full swing. All you have to do is be present and rise to the occasion.

Never be afraid to move on!

Remember that the DiVaz rid-o-meter is her very own intuition, not yo' best friendz, not yo' co-workerz and sometimes even yo' mamma has an agenda. Remember, If your heart says "NO," C'ya!

Most of us don't need to worry about getting mugged.

We beat ourselves up.

There is no such thing as failure in a relationship.

If you gave all that you could give, simply put,

He wasn't "The One."

Next!

ROCK BOTTOM

When DiVaz talk about "ROCK BOTTOM" they are usually referring to the tight buns you get in Yoga class or from countless hours at the gym. Unfortunately, this is not what I am referring to.

When you hit ROCK BOTTOM... Girlfriend, there ain't no mistakin' it for anywhere else. Let's get a perspective.

This entire book is about shifting your thinking and empowering yourself. If you think you have hit ROCK BOTTOM, switch up your game plan, honey! Obviously, nothing you have done thus far works. Why remain attached to it?

When your back is up against the wall...

turn around

face it

and

BREAK IT DOWN

17

This isn't deep.

**" So as the Phoenix has lifted itself from the ashes…
You too will fly again!"**

I find it ironic that those holding us back always seem to make it to the top and succeed. Irrespective of their personal definition of success. Perhaps it is a cosmic joke. **Whatever!**

It ain't funny! I wish them the best, but right now, I am concerned about you, DIVa. Why should you be the only one crying?

Find your true path.

Start doing fun things in your life… the things you've always wanted to do. Just send everyone in your life that You allowed to hold you back, yes… its your fault, out the door with the age old proverbial saying,

Let the doe knob hit ya, where the good Lord split ya!

Another way to put it rather succinctly is "Step Off!"

The sooner you let go...

The sooner you embrace your true destiny.

You do your thing while others get to do theirs.

Limitation gets the grande "Adios" from the scenario. In an extraordinary way, this is the birthplace of unconditional love. It is a never-ending circle of abundance and self-fulfilling prophecy, simply because, Duh...

"Everybody gets ta' do their own Thang!"

2

Been there...
Done that !

Never let anything new into your life
that remotely resembles anything
you just got rid of...

If you are Broke... Bored... or Buggared...

You can not trust your own judgement. You have programmed yourself to settle for less than you deserve and you make decisions for yourself that breed disaster. **Know that! Own that!**

We are directly responsible for all of our choices. We can blame no one but ourselves.

Analyze that!

Once you commit to the "New You," there is no turning back. Be a DIVa and fight for your life. When you make a decision that you are not certain of... Flip the script. If the flip side is congruent with DIVadom, then you know that it is tight and right.

Don't be daft... Run with it

When you free yourself from old patterns, you realign your balance. Tip the scale and lean into Fabulous! Motivate yourself to be healthy in mind, body and spirit. Why is it so easy to think negative when we can choose to think about something good? How many of us fall asleep at night worrying about bills, kids, work and HIM?

Use the time, just before you drift off to sleep, to be a Princess. In my dreams, I am a Flawless Movie Star. My favorite icons adore me. Tiger Woods worships me. Jude Law wants me to be his leading lady. Bill Gates keeps sending me gifts... really big diamonds. Tom Ford designs only for me. Greatest of all... I can actually fit the clothes.

Yes, dahling, bedtime is alright with me...

Every morning I wake up with a smile and I am ready to face the world. Okay so it's a pipe dream, but a DIVA counts on dreams coming true!

What is worse that worrying?

I think the only thing worse than worrying is

M iNDiNG SOMEBODY ELSE'S BUSiNESS

Stress triggers illness. Science validates this fact.

The mind is phenomenal. It is the first light of ideas.

If you think negative, you create negative.

You attract what you create in thought.

Words are power.

Words propel energy into action.

The impulse relays information to the cosmos and your dreams come to life. When you affirm the positive, you signal the universe to deliver goodness.

When I find that I am broke…

I remind myself that I am not broken.

I ignore the agonizing way I feel, when I am dangling over the edge, and I stand on my faith. I know that there is redemption. This energy places me on the precipice of a new plateau and I am no longer afraid to look down. I refer to it as,

"The glistening dawn of a new journey…"

I use this time to write. Ironically, writing is the hardest thing to do when you don't have money. The thought of unpaid bills kicks up on your ass like nothing else, however... being a DiVa-in-Training forces me to see the Phat side of the Power of Manifestation, a publishing deal.

When I am bored... I travel... Getting away does wonders for the soul. I go as far as I can afford to go. Recently, I went to the Renaissance Faire. It took me back to Elizabethan England. It was wonderful. I spoke Old English and bought some funky Fairy shoes. I wear them all over town. They are wild. Okay... so I ate veggie soup for a week. That, my friend, is not depravation. That my friend, is a DiVa diet.

Christmas and my birthday are 10 days apart. This is a difficult time of year for me. However, this year was a blast. I was determined to have an incredible holiday so I went to Amsterdam and hung out with friends. On the morning of my birthday, I called a friend in Venice and arrived in St. Marco's square in time for dinner.

Breakfast in the Netherlands... Cake and Champagne in a Gondola. I stayed through the New Year. That was awesome! So I ate veggie soup for 6 months. It was worth it!

Buggared is a British term.

I will leave it to you to find out exactly what it means if you don't already know. One can find themselves, Buggared... when things go massively awry.

Buggared is where you will find yourself if you don't adhere to the DiVaz commandment #2...

BEEN THERE... DONE THAT !

On this, I will say no more.

3

Free your mind and your ass will follow...

Defy Gravity by lifting the labels
and
open your life to transformation.

Strip away the labels that people place upon you and open your life to transformation. Trust, accept and know that Supreme empowerment governs DIVadom. Faith enables us to see beyond the things we don't understand.

Standing on our faith fortifies our belief system and assures us that everything is happening in our lives precisely as it should. Faith retains the alignment to the design. This makes the day to day grind easier to bear. Baby steps no longer appear to be tedious but actually begin to lead to...

All Things Fabulous.

Faith allows the true DIVa to laugh at life's struggles.
Even the stock market is Bear before it is Bullish!

Remove the **Player Haters** from your life.
So what if it causes a bit of a row!

Faith is the vessel of positive energy.
We are the channels through which it flows.

What happens next?

As we tear down the old city, we build a new one. We lay a new foundation with the design from your customized blueprints. Faith is the protective bubble that keeps us free from worry. Divine protection has no concerns because everything is taken care of. Free your mind from limited thinking. Move forward to accomplish great feats. Commit to uncontested integrity. Honor, respect, dignity and grace are the concrete. These are the qualities of nobility.

Set a standard for your new life as a DIVa.

Insist that Faith support it.

The ever- present, all knowing Supreme
will never let you fall

4

Make your dreams come true!

Ask
and
you shall receive...

How many times have you heard this before?

Don't be afraid to call upon the "DiVa within" to

Rise and Reveal Herself.

Ask for what you need and be specific.

There is a saying, "Be careful what you ask for"

the rest of that saying goes, "You just might get it."

Shall I elaborate... here goes.

Who on earth is going to hand you your dreams on a silver platter unless there is something in it for them? People in general are not that giving. Most people will not support your dreams because they don't have the courage to realize their own. How triflin' is that?

So, to whom can you turn to?

Go within, Darling.

Consult the DiVa.

What do you think she is there for?

How many times do I have to repeat myself!

Three No-Noz of Divadom

Would of, Should of, Could of!

You can not become a plastic surgeon with a beautician's license. Sometimes you have to bust your ass to make your dreams come true. Don't give up, the moment you do...

You are last year's Fashion

O u t !

Know this...

the essential component of loving ones' Self, is awakening to the realization that we deserve to win and be happy. The same God that created the Fabu Diva Julia Roberts, the adorable Diva Britney Spears and the Royal Diva Princess Diana created you too. I'd say, You, are in splendid company. You also descend from royal birth. You have talent, charisma and intelligence that no other on this earth expresses as you do.

In the business world, this is defined as Brand equity. Identify your market and work it like a nine to five until you turn a profit, girl.

Don't stop until you get enough.

Yesterday, I was bored and I decided that I wanted to go to a party. I was writing all day and the walls were closing in. There was only one problem, I had no plans, no invitations. A few moments later, my telephone rang and I was on my way.

The night was Off the Hook.

Irrespective of the party being "All That," I was proud of my power of manifestation working so quickly. Today, I asked for a wealthy, gorgeous, powerful and generous, available lover, who only has eyes for me, to appear on my doorstep. I am still waiting!

The night is young.

Commit to your dreams. Don't get frustrated with the timetable. Let the Goddess do her thing and deliver your dreams when you are ready to receive them.

Bloom from within and radiate an inner glow. Explore missed opportunities. Turn over every stone and seek its treasures.

Sail through life on cruise control and live it up.

Don't...

overload your circuits by taking on too much. Be easy on yourself. Ride the Wave. Remember that DIVaz are High Maintenance, spiritually speaking, that is why it takes a little longer for your dreams to come to fruition.

Create...

a consistent quality in your life. You will feel safe in the balance. Don't internalize the gray days. You may be a DIVa but you can not control the weather. Cloudy days fill the calendar for a reason. For those of you that don't get it... Cloudy days are present in our lives so we can appreciate the Sun.

Pace yourself...

always remember that dynasties rise and dynasties fall but there is no greater Dynasty than Miss Crystal Carrington and network syndication. One hit and you will be paid forever. Okay! This is an old school analogy, but it still works.

Now you work it, DIVa !

5

Put the "D" back in FUN. (FUNDz)

Plan your financial future
Create
an investment portfolio.

What is more fun than clothes shopping?
House hunting, Sister Girl!

The first time you pull up to a mansion that you can actually afford, you get a DiVa rush that is better than sex. I said a mansion that you can afford, not a gift from Daddy, not a gift from your man. You!

You don't have to be wealthy to invest. While I am not an expert, and certainly not an example, take it from 20/20 hindsight. Money, or the lack of it, is one of the greatest DiVa lessons there is. Trust me, you don't want to find out the hard way.

Do your homework to find the brokerage right for you. Some Online trades start as low as $ 8.00 per trade. Don't be embarrassed to call a broker.

The market is highly competitive now. Many reputable companies would love to have you as a client. They hold the expectation that your portfolio will blossom and you will remain loyal. Get the girls together and pool your pocket money. Select a portfolio that is safe, for the most part and steady in growth.

If you don't have a generous benefactor or trust fund waiting for you, **then you better get busy**. Save as much as you can.

What if you have no money to save?

When you have run out of **disguise,**

there is no room for **compromise,**

you desperately need to **revise,**

There is only one 𝒟𝒾𝒱𝒶 thing to do, **Improvise!**

There is no excuse not to have money. What talents do you have? Use your talents to devise a plan to generate income. I will teach you how to Brand yourself.

I don't mean go out and get a tattoo.

Suppose you are an excellent cook. A good gage would be all of the neighborhood kids hanging around your house at dinnertime. Start a food club. Prepare lunches for the kids to take to school and deliver dinners to the neighbor's houses for a fee, of course.

If you start a **Grub Club**, you can charge a membership fee. (Make sure you check with City Hall for guidelines.) Print out a weekly menu and distribute it to enhance excitement. Check to see if your members have common likes and dislikes. Please them and they will always come back for more. On the weekends, you can teach a cooking class at home.

If you have enough original recipes to fill a book, write one.

Next step, go to a manufacturer and pitch a line of frozen foods.

Soon you will be able to buy the **Grub Club** product line in a super market near you.

Can you hear **Chi Ching!**

Don't laugh, the big stars do it all the time.
All you need is a publicist and a new dress.

Think Martha Stewart!

You will be surprised to find out how many people are willing to pay you. If they are not, move on. I equate getting paid with respect.

The most important thing to keep at the forefront of the quest is to have fun. If you can't see the path clearly to financial freedom...

Still yourself and check in with the DIVa

She will speak to you softly and let you know what to do next. Live your life from limitless space and see beyond the shortcomings that are illusion. You can't believe a little bit. You can't love a little bit.

All or nothing is a phrase of the past.

It's all and everything, DIVa!

The term "Nothing" exists in the past.
Don't even joke about it.

Use your words and your power of manifestation to Rise!

6

On Men...
Forgive them
for they know not what they do!

Even if they are Rocket Scientists
or
Brain Surgeons,
when it comes to understanding women…

Forget about it!

Generally speaking, men don't have a clue when it comes to women. (note, I said generally) Although the DiVaz perspective on her male counterpart could fill the vast virtual space spanning the World Wide Web, we will still start with the obvious.

Why would you trust anyone with your life
and
most importantly your heart?

If the Creator wanted us to entrust our hearts and our lives to another, He would have gone to greater lengths with care.

He would have encoded a serial number that matched His, our preordained **"Lord Protector."**

Consider the notion of a cosmic liability policy that would insure against attracting the wrong mate. You would know that the laundry list of **boy toyz** was just that and no more.

As we sail along together across this uncharted sea, we will discover that men all over the world vibrate to the same energy. (generally speaking, of course!)

Man are really quite simple. Man all want to eat, or depending on class and upbringing, shovel large quantities of unidentifiable rot into their dark abyss. They all want to shag, fart and without further adieu, roll over and fall asleep.

What is remarkably impressive... so do we.

Women just want it to be romantic.
We want to feel special.

Women want Men to hang on to our every word and worship us. I've got news for you, honey! While they may pretend that they are genuinely present when we are having our little chats, trust me when I tell you, they are instant replaying, the last great moments of the NBA championship series in their heads. That's why they stare into the distance pensively, clear their throats and try to hold back that silly little grin, which on an expert can sometimes be mistaken for an,

"Air of concern."

The only reason they listen in the first place is because you provide access to the "gaping portal of Schtuppdom." The Fountain that quenches their carnal thirst.

So, why bother? Isn't that a silly question? I hope none of y'all are out there asking this question.

DiVaz aren't male bashers! It would take me three lifetimes to exalt and sing the praises of men.

Men are Fabu!
DiVaz Dig Dudes!

If you can not conjure up accolades for them and all else fails, honey... think fireworks. If nothing else rings a bell, go with the Baseball analogy. Trust me, when a real man steps up to bat, batteries can not duplicate the Grand Slam.

In the spirit of equity and fairness, men come along with their own set of baggage and drama. The difference is, women lay out problems on a table like a potluck at a PTA meeting and men keep everything locked inside, hoping that the "Way out" will present itself through osmosis.

Men are also trying to fulfill a destiny, live full lives, and leave their mark on the pages of history. Then the real world steps in, kicks them in the ass, and chuckles in their face rather loudly and rudely, just as it does us.

Then you come along, Miss DiVa, sashaying your pretty little behind, all up in the middle of his world, wanting to rearrange everything. Pheromones start flying and love looks him straight in the eyes.

Most men can not deal with one of these events, let alone a Big Mac combo or shall I say, a Mac Daddy combo. What makes you think he can sort out his life, rescue yours and keep both of you happy? Even if he wants to, it's asking too much.

Why don't you meet him half way?

Give him a chance to discover himself through his reflection in you. Allow love to reveal itself naturally, in small doses. Don't burn out the flame. Fan the fire by allowing him to slowly drink the elixir that is expressly "YOU." Let him grow in confidence. Let it feel good when he is with you. Let him feel safe in the pace of the progression. He will either "Step Up or Step Down.

Either way... You're still a DiVa. To his friends...

A legend!

Never give anything away,
        you wish you could take back later!

Hootchie Mama or Gucci Mama!

You are much too Fabulous
and much too Flawless
to give away the "Jewels" on a maybe…

Think of life and love as the ultimate game. Think of sex as the trump card. Why would you play it, if you weren't absolutely certain you could win? This is not to say that sex is a tool or a weapon to get what you want. However, a large percentage of you DiVaz-in- training use it in this regard, so we might as well address it.

There is no exchange of energy without consequence. Love travels beyond space and time, over multiple reincarnations to spark anew. Our communion, through the gift of love making, is bound to a karmic response that sets into motion an irrevocable path. It triggers information that supports or challenges our Spiritual DNA.

If the feedback is negative, it sends that signal out into the universe and you attract all that is drawn from a vibration that is devoid of light. It manifests in a spectrum of ill -fated energy.

If you need a list, start with sexual transmitted diseases, unwanted pregnancy, far worse, unloved children. If that isn't enough...

What about a broken heart ?

DiVaz must learn to protect their investment by playing their hand close. Never let anyone see what you are holding. There is nothing wrong with waiting to see where the chips may fall. If he loves you, he will fight for you. Then and only then do you show him what cards you are holding. Always remember,

"Forbidden fruit is the sweetest."

If you enjoy the casual air of a clandestine alliance or a midnight rendezvous also known as the "Booty Call," know that there is always a price to pay eventually. Think of it as a fierce wind that blows into your life and sweeps away your life force. It leaves you standing alone on a barren field looking at the empty pages of your life. Where is the victory in that? For some, the reward is the temporary gratification. I guess that's okay, if you can deal with it.

My Diva-o-meter is far too precise for intimate rejection.

Why waste your energy if he is not, "The One!" Which reverts to the original point, Why would you give the most precious expression of your higher being to someone that does not give you in return their undying love? It leaves an imprint on our subconscious and the cumulative repercussion of "Dangerous Liaisons" is simply this, it short-circuits and delays " True Love." In order to share the rest of your life with " The One,"

You must be "The One."

Without integrity, dignity and respect,

you are nothing.

Rising to temperance and standing on indelible faith while whole-heartedly believing, "The One is on the way," lets the universe know you are ready to receive.

When you begin to root the foundation of your life in self-defined integrity, the 'DiVa' that "Rises from within" will not allow you to play games. She will not permit you to do anything that sets you back. She will not allow room for regret by not allowing you to create it.

Love can not be found because it is never lost.

It circulates throughout all things from its Divine source.
It is an emanation of the Supreme.

It's your call.

Either you are a Hootchie Mama or a Gucci Mama!

8

The Three Cardinal sins of Divadom:

Depression, Regression, and Obsession

No... No... and Hell No!

THINK DIVA!

Depression is a lowly state of mind that affects every aspect of our life. It is a choice that we make to look at ourselves from the perspective of lack and limitation. It is a destructive environment that builds an intense wall around us. Nothing gets in. Nothing goes out. It is a vacuum. You can not breathe in a space devoid of air. You can not see a landscape that is silhouetted in darkness.

Why would you go there?

Why is it so much easier to worry and hang out in a disenchanted energy than to think positive?

It is my opinion, that the greatest trick the Creator played on mankind was granting the gift of Free Will ! We have the irrevocable right, sanctioned to us from the Highest of Highs, to think as we choose. Are you with me? Okay, so, if mankind is created in the image and likeness of the Creator, which by definition, is a constant state of Infinite Love, boundless, pure and perfect; what does that make us?

It makes us general partners with the Divine. This is not a limited partnership where we only get to share in the rewards minimally. This is a life time guarantee that "Every day is the day!" **Seen…**

In order to remove depression from your existence, a *DIVa* must start with this basic truth. The Supreme energy that grants all desires, that protects us, that embraces us, that empowers us, that inspires and fulfills us, that loves us and bestows upon us the gift of love… is within.

Focus on this great light.

When you are feeling low,

know that it is a feeling

and not a state of life.

It will pass. It is a side effect of temporary circumstances that have been set before you. When you find yourself moving toward depression, try to identify the cause and address it before it takes hold. Is it money, loneliness, boredom? The list goes on. Don't dwell on it. Fix it. Divas decide what makes them happy. Go after it with a vengeance. Devise a plan to alleviate the depression. Put it into action. You will be so busy moving in this new direction that you will not have time to regress.

Regression is an unnatural motion

that propels us backward.

It is a downward spiral into a perpetual state of limitation. It is the side kick of depression. Depression and regression are conjoined. Where you find one, you will undoubtedly find the other. If you find yourself regressing, go back to the DiVaz commandments #1 and #2.

The DiVaz space is a place where limitations do not exist. We know that the Creator grants all. We know that all we must do is claim it.

Drama is simply a distraction.

Problems are cosmic barometers to help us identify our true desires by magnifying what we don't want. Claim what you do want and affirm your Divine right to receive by taking the steps necessary to make your dreams come true.

Shine forth that unwavering light of the Supreme...

no matter what.

You will reign victorious.

The simple act of shifting your mind to positive thought will burn away all that creates depression.

Let the Creator do the rest.

You should not let a day go by without first acknowledging and thanking God for the little things. They are the things that we take for granted. When I am feeling low, I look for that tiny light that flickers in the smallest of Miracles. When you have nothing, it is difficult to feel loved because we as humans place a tremendous value on material things. When you have nothing, you feel slighted, unimportant, and worthless.

Look around you and you will see the gifts that the Creator has given you. This will assure you that the great destiny indelibly printed on your life is on its way. We all start on different paths in life to arrive at the same end. It is not a race. The challenge is within. Each of us must "Rise above the Self." We must "Rise above the ego" that has welcomed vanity, greed, and selfishness. Clear the path so the true DiVa, that you know you are, can step up and

Make Her Entrance!

When I referred to the dictionary to define obsession, my findings were frightening. It means "to haunt" or "to fill the mind." I took it a step further to define the word, "haunt." Aside from the ghostly reference, it means, "to resort to habitually" or a "place of frequent resort." The DiVa definition refers to "the return to a state that is devoid of Grace."

There is a difference between a DiVa mission

and an obsession

A DiVa mission is a goal, which has been set, once all of the elements, both pro and con, have been factored into the equation.

In short, you have searched your heart for right of cause. To define this further, your decisions must be determined by integrity, honor and respectability. You must also consider how your decisions affect those involved as well.

DiVaz must learn to take responsibility
        for the repercussion or reward of accomplishment.

The easiest way to identify an obsession from a
                DiVa mission is to defer to the definition of Grace.

Grace =
self-esteem,
discernment
refined motion,
and Divine favor.

If you pursue anything that does not embody every attribute of Grace, it is a waste of time.

Nothing good will come of it.

If you compromise your integrity, honor, or respectability...

Nothing good will come of it.

If you go after it anyway or place this notion in a high place, and this notion pervades your noble state of mind...

you know you are being shady...

This is an obsession!

Don't go there!

Men and money are oftentimes at the forefront of a woman's obsession. Without a proper understanding of the balance between when to fight and when to yield, you will always attract the ingredients for failure. You may win a few, here and there, but you will always find yourself stuck, somewhere short of ecstasy. Frustration sets in because you have to start all over again.

Aren't you tired of struggle?

Struggle = misplaced energy.

You know in your heart of hearts when something is worth fighting for, don't you? Reserve yourself for the battles worth winning. Walk away from the rest. Gracefully, of course! The most powerful tool a DIVa possesses is her ability to think. Thinking clearly replaces worry.

THINK DIVAZ !

When your back is up against the wall...
turn around
face it
and

BREAK IT DOWN !

Does this sound familiar?

9

Sense and Sensibility...

Never leave the house without looking flawless;
for sure, you will run into
"Him!"

Sense, Scents, and Sensibility...
What's a girl to do?

So many DiVa lessons and so little time. Let's refer again to the Master of literal precision, Webster. Again we are astounded. He identifies "Sense" as consciousness, coherent or intelligible meaning.

In DiVa terminology, to use one's sense defers to the employment of the faculty of reason and perception working together in delicate harmony. Once you can rely on your brain to think clearly without impulsive repercussion and your heart speaks to you honestly, without judgement of Outcome, you are ready to go.

You can conquer anything!

A DIVa must also rely on her senses, particularly her sixth sense and her sense of smell. If you are in hot pursuance of a trail that emanates a scent that smells anything like elephant droppings, why would you continue the pursuit? You wouldn't! Follow your nose.

Good things smell good. You can not always trust your senses, especially when it comes to men. Your senses run on auto-pilot when it comes to Hotteez, but if you sniff around long enough, they begin to wreak if they are stinkers!

Every DIVa knows that sensibility can be equated to style. When you are confident that your internal guide is working at an optimal performance level, you feel on top of your game. You feel sexy, sensuous, attractive and powerful. The DIVa definition of "all of the above" is... **Glamorous!**

An aspect of sensibility is the way we respond or behave in any given situation. I will not lecture you on manners. I am certain your mother has taught you something. However, I will leave you with these profound words of wisdom from the all-knowing voice of the DiVa...

Never leave your house without
flawless makeup,
flawless hair,
and a DiVa outfit...
for sure you will run into "HiM."

Nine things men hate about relationships
that Divaz never do...

Lies

Nagging

Possessiveness

Boring Sex

Sermons

TV Dinners

Frivolous Spending

Temper Tantrums

Your Girlfriend's Opinions

From a cosmic point of view, I would order the nine things not to do in this fashion: lies, nagging, possessiveness, sermons, frivolous spending, boring sex, cynicism and your girlfriends' opinions.

From a man's point of view, I would order them as follows: boring sex, frivolous spending, TV dinners... it doesn't matter how you prioritize the rest of the list. If you ain't keeping him satisfied or feeding him, you best not be spending up all his money, shopping. The rest of the list doesn't matter.

It's probably over anyway.

Let's dissect this from both perspectives, the cosmic point of view and practicality, that is, the mechanism of reason men employ to process information.

On Lies

The Cosmic Vibe: When you lie, you defile the part of yourself that has vowed to anchor this relationship in integrity. Lies, like all things negative, carry with it a charge of repercussion.

Where have you heard this before?

We've been through this already!

You can not run from what is true and good. It will always Rise to present itself. When you lie, you are deprived of your right to align with the force of truth. Since, I always feel compelled to break it down:

When you are busted
you get dissed!

The truth is so much sexier. When a *DIVA* finds herself in a difficult situation, she must choose her moment to present her case. Keep a soft controlled tone in your voice and just spit out the truth. The sooner you get it out, the better.

It's all in the performance anyway, Honey!
When that curtain goes up,
you best be workin' for the Oscar.

In the event you are prone to digging yourself into a deeper mess... don't do a lot of explaining. Wait for a response.

If he senses your sincerity, you will be forgiven.

Count on your man Rising to the honest part of you that respects him so much, you protect him, even when you have everything to lose.

Forgiveness is the reward of honesty.

When the Gucci is on the other foot,
Divaz always forgive.

Okay, now let's flip the coin. From his point of view, if you start lying, yo' man reserves the right to lie also. Except his lies are usually bigger and more devastating. His lies usually involve HER !

Train your man to be honest with you by not reacting to him negatively when he opens up to you. You may not like everything you hear, but at least you get a glimpse of his intellectual mechanics.

Play your hand close until you can see all the cards on the table. Oh and don't forget to rely on your sixth sense and your sense of smell!

On Nagging

It's simple. From a cosmic point of view, it relinquishes your power to another. Do you enjoy listening to someone ranting?

No!

Nagging doesn't work. The natural response is to tune it out. If something vexes you, let him know. Say it without whining. If he keeps it up and it affects your happiness, surely you know what to do by now,

"Let him go."

On Possessiveness

When one is possessive of another, it screams out to the world, "Hey, look at me, I am insecure and I am not worthy." DIVaz don't vibrate to this. Life as a DIVa is a constant whirlwind of pursuit. To be pursued by the crème de la crème is her 9 to 5.

Why would you chase a man? Why would you try to tie him down? As soon as he catches you off guard... the instant he spots an opening, he is out of there.

Jealousy generates "The Bolt!"
also known as
the Male's Primal Leaving Dance.

In addition, anything that infringes upon his freedom, sporting events, or his night out with the boyz, invokes **"The Bolt."**

So how does a woman protect herself from feeling unprotected and unloved? How would you respond to this situation? He wants to go out with the boyz. You want him to spend time with you. Here are your three choices for the correct answer.

1) Let him know how important it is for you to spend time together, and ask him nicely if he could stay home with you instead of going out with the boyz.

2) Pick a man that actually has a clue, that you... DiVa, are his priority, not the boyz, so you don't have to ask. He knows when you need him.

3) If he ignores your feelings and he goes out anyway, get dressed up, look incredible and go out with the girlz. Make sure you leave first and he sees you leave so he can experience the "empty silence."

The answer is number two. Who wants to feel unloved? If you have followed the commandments and chosen "The One," he gets it. You don't have to do anything except keep making each other happy. You know when to ask him to stay; you know when to leave him alone.

Number 1 and 3 are also correct in their respective circumstances. Maybe you two have been together for a while and everything is becoming routine. Men are sometimes content in simplicity. Men don't always realize they have to do anything to make you happy. Coming home is enough. A gentle nudge never hurts.

If he chooses not to listen and take heed, a gentle warning is in order. When words don't seem to work anymore, a DIVa must let her actions speak louder. Get dressed up and go out. Stay out a little later than he does. Let him know that you are sorry, the time just got away from you. You also let him know how much fun you had. Kiss him sweetly, roll over and go to sleep.

On Boring Sex

What is that?

I am only guessing on this one because I don't know anything about boring sex. However, it is my opinion that this is the number one "No, No" for a *Diva*. If you are lucky enough to share your life with "The One," where else should he go to exchange this energy. You know you would go **BUCK WILD** if he went outside the relationship. So why would you put your "Sugar Love Daddy" in that position? It would be your fault if he cheated, not his.

In the beginning of a relationship, when love is new, all you *Divaz* out there could write your very own version of "How to Please Yo' Man." However, once most women are committed and real life sets in... bills, kids, routine... you know the drill; it is hard to "Rise to the Occasion."

My theory... less is more. Making love is much better when you are both present. Passion is so beautiful. It is harder to find when you wear it out all the time. That gets old. Enjoy each other. Talk, laugh, caress... Intimacy does not exist in the performance.

Men know when you are faking it. DiVaz don't fake. DiVaz actually love pleasing their man all the time. (I can not believe I just wrote that!) Yes, girl it is work, but someone has got to do it. That someone is you!

An old granny saying is, "You made your bed, now you have to lay in it." It means we have to be responsible for the choices we make. When you choose love, you have to be willing to Rise to love. He no doubt will want to! (chuckle, chuckle)

On Sermons

Sermons... if your man wants to listen to a preacher, he should go to church. There is nothing more unattractive than self-righteous indignation and judgment.

If you want to run him out of your life...
keep running your mouth.

Cynicism is unattractive. It is also condescending by the nature of its definition. Sermons are eulogies. If you strip a man of all that he is, right or wrong, he is no longer a man. Remember that he has a destiny to fulfill also. He has a path to follow and lessons to learn. Let him grow at his own pace. If you love freely, he will be the man you intuitively recognize him to be.

If you think your burnin' hunk of love needs a Mommy instead of a lover, you should have thought about that before you got involved.

You don't pick fruit and eat it before it is ripe, do you? So, don't get involved with someone that is not ready to fully commit to you.

Share your opinions only if they are welcomed. If they are not, always encourage and support any positive decisions your man makes. Don't inspect them for *Outcome*. Don't critique them. Uplift him and reassure him that you trust his choices.

Never make him feel inadequate. I am not talking about big stuff like important "life" and "family" stuff. I am just talking about "His Stuff."

If it is necessary to break it down…

Don't cut off his ballz!"

On TV Dinners

Do not feed your man fast food. What is it made of anyway? Learn to cook. Anybody can cook these days thanks to Martha Stewart and the Food Channel. There is no excuse. Make cooking something that you do together. Make it sensual.

Just feed him, Honey. Every Italian man I know always makes it home for dinner. If you have experienced the splendor of dining with an Italian family, you will know what I mean. Every night is a feast. Food is a shared expression of love and the fastest way to his heart...

So put your best Gucci forward and Work it!

On Frivolous Spending

Frivolous spending is bad news if your man doesn't have a lot of money. It is the fast track to disaster. If you require luxury, make sure you have enough money of your own. If you do not have enough money to support your habit and a man with money is high on your "I do" list, Don't pick a man that does not have any. This is basic curriculum, " DiVa 101." That would be "Toopid!" (the 4 years old pronunciation of stupid)

On Temper Tantrums

Temper tantrums, once invoked, can escalate into abuse. If you abuse him, he could retaliate with the same reaction. Verbal abuse is just as painful as violence. When you lose respect for each other and have a break down in communication, ruin is imminent.

If you are high strung and you can't control your emotions, leave. Go for a walk... cool down, but don't "Go off."

If you choose to "Go off," you will be sorry
                    and you may end up on Jerry Springer.

Divaz don't do Jerry!

On Your Girlfriend's Opinions

Who cares what your girlfriends think! Most of them are living in a bad episode of "Sex in the City." They didn't help you capture your man's heart. You did that all on your own. So why would you run back to him and give him a piece of her mind on anything that happens in your bed?

Trust me... he does not want to hear it. He will either grow to resent her or he will resent you.

Friends don't fly free...
Tell them to keep their asses home!

Dramalogue for Divaz

Miracles exist on the horizon of change.

Trouble equals Free will defying Intuition.

Patience... the moment one accepts

the comings and goings of life

while appreciating the solace in between

To be or not to be is not the question.

It is how far you are willing to go to...
succeed

The noble victor knows
when to put down the sword
and walk away from the battle

Unhealthy energy disables
and
forbids us to function

Feng Shui Your Life

The breath of life that connects all things to the Supreme force is known as "Chi."

Chi is the thread that runs through all things visible and invisible. It connects us to a universal power line.

Think of it as cosmic electricity.

When you turn on a lamp that is plugged into a charged socket, you get light. This is not possible without the electricity. Without the electricity, all you have is a lamp with the capability to shine forth light. It can not illuminate without the power of electricity.

Whether or not you turn on the switch, the electricity is alive, although it is inactive or in reserve.

Chi, like electricity is ever present in nature. It possesses similar qualities to air and electricity in the sense that its flow can be blocked or stifled. It can affect every aspect of our lives, health, love, fortune etc. The abundance of "All Goodness" is apparent when Chi flows freely. The opposite occurs when it does not.

Chinese Masters and healers reveal to us the mystery of the art of balancing Chi. Westerners have gone "Feng Shui" crazy in their effort to align the energy in their homes with the force of Chi.

This is the basis of Feng Shui, the alignment of Chi to invoke balance and good fortune.

It is so comprehensive that I dare not expound upon it further. If you wish to know more, consult a Master, or check out some of the numerous books and web sites available on this ancient wisdom that is fast becoming a modern trend.

The embodiment of Feng Shui can also apply to life. All we have to do is clear out the blockage and plug into the energy provided by the Supreme force. Chi flows throughout the human body via the Chakras. There are seven "points of entry" into the physical body through which Chi can flow. Without getting heavy, Chi connects our ethearic impression, which is our invisible carbon copy, to the Body, which in turn binds us to the source, Supreme energy.

This is not a complicated journey.

When it is broken down to its lowest common denominator, we can clearly identify it as binary.

Are you # 1
Or
Are you a zero?

Are you a winner?

Or

Do you exist in the vague haze of mediocrity?

The first step to connecting to the "Power of Chi" is to acknowledge that it exists.

The second step is to examine your life to be certain that you are qualified to chart and navigate your course.

The third step is to "Boldly go where none have gone before!"

Once you get going, you will get so excited, your hooters will start to twirl! Nothing will stop you and none will stand in your way.

How do we get there?

By adapting the basic principles of Chi

as they apply to the

The Tao of the Diva.

Mind over Matter

The mastery of self-reliance is evident in one who fine-tunes the ear to the whisper of the heart. All truth resides within and here lies one of the principle Chakras. It is known as the "Heart Chakra."

Chi enters the heart and sends the charge, which vibrates, to reason over sentiment, logic over feeling. When we listen to the inner voice and honestly yield to its resolve in earnest, it will never lead us astray. Learn to trust and rely on this voice for guidance. Even when it goes against the grain of all others and you stand alone.

Know that you are not alone because you are protected by your Divine Heritage. As you become confident, you build fortitude. The courage to stand alone in the face of adversity and fear is granted.

Fortitude reinforces integrity. Once integrity kicks in, you are no longer willing to compromise that which is founded in truth.

This is the first step along the path to transcendence. It is the "first light" of wisdom. The questions of the past now present themselves as answers... Revelation.

This is the way of the Buddha.

In order to remove the blockage of Chi, one must employ the protective power of truth. Free-flowing Chi is synonymous with the ability to possess sovereignty over negative thinking and this ain't always easy, yet it is imperative that every DIVA holds this discipline in high esteem.

Thoughts and ideas also resonate to Chi. Thoughts signal the intellect to manifest radiance, illuminating Chi or they cast a stagnating shadow, dimming Chi.

The weight and measure of ones' strengths and weaknesses is paramount to the understanding of the Self.

How can you know which course of action to take if you don't evaluate your threshold of endurance?

Here is a Divaz checklist for decision making:

Is this what I really want?

Am I being selfish?

Will it hurt me in the end?

Will I hurt others?

What can I learn from this if I fail?

What is the path I shall take to achieve this goal?

Is it realistic?

Can I handle this task and go the distance?

Is the timing right?

The power to ascertain your personal threshold of endurance, protects us from biting off more than we can chew. When we truly comprehend the overview of a mission, it grants us peace of mind because we know it is manageable.

When the mind is serene, we create.

Uneasiness is a clear gage that something is out of balance. Always remember, it is okay to rethink the plan. True DiVaz know when to retreat, and when to launch a new plan of attack.

The Dissipation of Chi

How many mornings do you wake up, look in the mirror, and say to yourself, "Why bother getting up, nothing good is going to happen to me today. Who cares about me anyway?"

When you can sense a void in your life, this is the "Diva within" crying out to come forth. Not only are we "Drama and Trauma Queens," we are also "Tragedy Queens." Divaz play all the parts, honey!

When we feel hopeless because the man of our dreams hasn't shown up yet. Instead of a hero, we keep meeting the zero. When we feel unloved because the man of our dreams ain't acting right.

When the funds are low and you don't have any dough. When you feel old because all of the women on TV look like refugees from a MTV video, This is a dissipation of Chi.

Your purpose on this planet must not be measured by the standard of another set beside you for comparison, nor is your destiny defined by *Outcome*. *Outcome* defines the intended result of an action.

Most of us relate to a definition of *Outcome* as the prosperous and auspicious result of a predetermined positive action. That is why we feel disappointment when things don't go our way. *Outcome* and expectation are side effects of attachment.

It is the intrinsic nature of attachment to create imbalance because attachment is a victim of circumstance. You can not carry out an action and be absolute in respect to its *Outcome*. You can only estimate the return on your investment.

Once you designate energy to propel an action into being, all of the variables must also be factored into the equation.

The universe factors all considerations into the process of a response. All responses to actions are individually designed.

You are the determining factor!

Your Destiny carefully masterminds the design. This is why you can not question Outcome. Even sudden wealth can be destructive if we are not ready to receive it spiritually. Know that the hand dealt to you is the perfect one for you. One must not waste their true cause or purpose through the employment of doubt.

So...

How does the DiVa "Rise" out of the depths, when each time you try harder, you are set back two steps?

Divaz rely upon the wisdom of Impermanence for it is the ebb and flow of all things.

Impermanence is the ever-evolving transience of all things. It is equally, "that which is real and that which is illusion." It is the motion of one thought as it tranforms into another. It is likened to the life cycle of growth and change, while it is also the perpetual spiritual quest to attain enlightenment.

Note that I said the "Quest" because in respect to wisdom there is no true achievement of it. I find it difficult to explain Impermanence. For me, it is my Sanctuary of peace where I require no resolution or response. I feel surrounded by a sea of calm that protects me from that which I can not comprehend. Yet, it is the open door to all comprehension.

The desire to achieve freedom from the "Dissipation of Chi" is paramount while on the path to the goal.

What have we learned?

Release the attachment to Outcome!

Stay with me now…

I know some of you are reluctant to vibe this when the bills are due or you are sitting around the house without a man, alone.

Dig this…

Once you master the understanding of attachment and impermanence, you have arrived. You will see the light.

The light is you… Diva.

What happens next?

Everything falls into place.

C'est Magique!

Rejection versus Selection

In case that went in one ear and out the other,

Rock with this!

You finally meet the man of your dreams and you have been dating successfully. You think all is well when suddenly, he decides to break it off because he is not ready for a commitment.

Or...

You are one negotiation away from clinching your dream job. The bills will finally get paid and you can sleep at night for a change. The next morning the telephone rings and it is the Human Resource department calling to say the boss' girlfriend got the job.

Where is the justice in that?

Moreover, where is Divine Intervention? What is up with all this Chi that is supposed to be overflowin' with abundance?

Rejection and disappointment are so powerful that they can demolish your entire belief system in a single stroke. It is so disastrous you just can't wait to say,

"I knew this Diva stuff was rubbish!"

Drama Queens unite!

Stand up and fight for what is rightfully yours by calling upon the "Diva within" to clear a path to that which has been ordained for you.

When Divaz are rejected,
Divaz don't cry.

Divaz only do tears when they are accepting awards.

CHAOS is defined as,
"The Creator Healing All things Obstructing Success."

When rejection is apparent, DiVaz immediately give thanks to the Supreme. This acknowledges the validation of the presence of the Divine working on our behalf.

Okay, so you already knew this.
Perhaps...
but you didn't really believe it when it mattered most.
If you did, you would not have bought this book!

Rejection is my new Buddy. It means, I don't have to be bothered with people that get on my nerves. I don't have to feel bad when a relationship doesn't work out. I know he is not meant for me, even though he is really hot. I don't have to indulge others with small talk hoping they will accept me. I hate small talk. I also don't have to work in a hostile environment anymore. My life is good!

What do we have to do to get here?

Nothing... just Chill!

The next time you stare rejection in the face,

$\qquad\qquad\qquad\qquad$ **Give it the finger!**

Know that your girl, the Diva,
and
a whole lot of Chi, have your back.

Look for the open door.

It is always there.

Now, Go on with Yo' bad self...

The Subconscious Sabotage of Love

There is not a DiVa in the vast realm of DiVadom that has not experienced a dysfunctional exchange of emotions. If you think you have not... count up all your ex- boyfriends or for some of y'all, ex-husbands, and you can see for yourself that you are not exempt. I sit high on the throne of this one.

Let's define sabotage.

In brief, it is intentional demise.
(Sorry, I don't have my dictionary handy.)

There is no reason for us to be alone or lonely. This is an imposed state of being. Everyone is entitled to be loved, happy and in love. There is just one catch.

Every man you let into your life, ain't "The One."

"The One is The One!

Instead of a massive thrashing about how we set ourselves up for failure in a relationship from a spiritual perspective, I will just list the things that are dead giveaways for DiVaz. You can feel "Toopid" later!

He's overweight but you think he would really be "Hot" if he went to the gym.

He has a handsome face, if only he could grow hair.

You would marry him, if he were a doctor instead of a plumber.

If only he wasn't so cheap, he would be your Prince.

You could really trust him if he would stop cheating.

Okay, so he's wealthy, handsome and a workaholic. You could really feel secure with him if he spent more time with you and stopped jet- setting all around the globe without you.

Subconscious sabotage is contagious.
Here are some of the signs.

If you are lonely and you are dating just to get out of the house. Okay, so he's not your type, but he's nice. Be careful. You are vulnerable. Most guys get the goods on this one. Once you open up to "Less than" you settle for less.

Another example, your clock is ticking and all your friends are married with children. Maybe he is not your dream guy but he is stable, so you consider marriage.

Are you out of your mind?

YES, girlfriend… you are 100% certifiable!

Go back to the Diva commandments.

I could go on and on with a list of examples, but you know when your booty stinks! You don't need me to point it out.

If you have dreamed all your life of "The One," why would you settle for "What's His Name!"

When water is still, it is clear. When it is disturbed, it is muddy. When you compromise love and he isn't, "The One," You are stirrin' up the mud and it is only a matter of time before your life is headed for a wreck.

You are drinkin' and drivin' down the highway of your life.

Subconscious sabotage can not exist when we truly know ourselves and believe that dreams come true. When you know yourself, you can go to dinner with "What's His Name, even take him home if you want, but it goes no further.

I ain't Granny, honey, I can't tell you how to do your thang. I can only express that which does not work for the DIVA. The rest is your call.

What is subconsciously sabotaging you?

What is holding you back?

THiNK DiVAZ !

We settle for less, when we don't believe that we deserve "True Love."

We settle for less when we don't believe that someone could love us as much as we could love another.

We settle for less when we feel destiny is taking too long.

We settle for less when we give our power away in exchange for short-term gratification.

We settle for less when we don't make safe decisions for ourselves.

We settle for less when we ponder the question,

"Is it ever gonna be my turn?"

Subconscious sabotage is rooted in fear. Once it takes hold, it can run away with all of your hopes and dreams.

If you allow it to live... Kiss your dreams "Good Bye."

One last footnote:

Enjoy your life, by staying in the driver's seat and don't drive drunk down the highway that leads you to your destiny.

Now, Slip on those Gucci's
and
Step out into the world.

The One"

I bet some of you opened the book and went straight to this chapter without even looking at the other chapters. Trying to find yo' man!

If you are looking for a shortcut, I am happy to disappoint you. You will thank me for it later. If your "Dream Guy" is all that you imagined he would be… you better be ready for him when he presents himself or you won't be secure enough to "Rise" and share your life with him. So, go back to the beginning of the book and catch up with the rest of us Divaz-in-training later. For those of you who are ready to,

"Go forth into the night!"

How do we know when he is "The One?"

Some DiVaz believe in "Love at First Sight." Some DiVaz enjoy sure and steady growth into a loving relationship. Some DiVaz can't stand his ass in the beginning, only to fall madly in love.

Love just happens!

There is no right or wrong way to fall in love.

True love is a right of passage. When it graces you with its presence, You feel like "You have Arrived." In this sense true love is a destination. However, it is not an *Outcome*. Love is a beginning without an end.

While it has the power to span lifetimes, cross space and time, it is ever-changing, therefore it is in a constant state of motion... Impermanent.

Love can only exist in complete freedom. You can't buy a ticket, catch it at a matinee, walk out of the theatre and have Russell Wong come home with you. Although, he feels real to you, you are not real to him... Okay, so get a grip!

True Love can not be inherited through a legacy.

You can't win it in a lottery.

You can be "Super fine and have all the riches in the world," but you still may not ever find "True Love".

Out of all of the things DiVaz "Must Be" or "Must not Be," she must be in love and loved or she will always pine for it.

True love is an essential component of the Diva.

All DiVaz are granted "The Divine Right of Love."

The Supreme knows this dear so,

Take a deep breathe and calm down.

Don't be so dramatic!

The Beatitudes

The **"Be" attitude** is the DiVaz power that "Rises" from within to resonate the beauty of your reflection as it pertains to true love.

True love will only come forth when you radiate true love. True Love
is our mirror reflection of our Divine relationship with the Creator. It is
the union of the

"God Man" and "Goddess Diva."

So the question should not be....

Is he The One?   Are you the One?

I will leave you with one final thought.

When you know he is The One,

It is this you know of yourself...

The Power of Love

You know he is "The One"
when you know of yourself...

The thought of him graces every part of you
as if it were the first stroke of a master
upon an empty canvas.

The Intoxication of Love

You know he is "The One"
when you know of yourself...

The touch of fate is irresistible.

It wraps you in its arms

and holds you like the golden clasp

on a string of pearls.

The Compassion of Love

You know he is "The One"
when you know of yourself...

The light shining bright within you
will never cast a shadow upon him
when he has lost his way.

The Emancipation of Love

You know he is "The One"
when you know of yourself...

His path has led him to your door

that will always remain open so that

he may come and go as destiny calls.

The Selfless Face of love

You know he is "The One"
when you know of yourself...

you would never ask him

to destroy within himself,

that which is essential

to the

realization

of his Divine purpose.

The Perpetual Motion of Love

You know he is "The One"
when you know of yourself...

that love unto itself is breath

to be inhaled and released.

Although it sustains life,

It can not exist apart from the *Self.*

The Ecstasy of Love

You know he is "The One"
when you know of yourself...

that passion is the only thirst
that can never be quenched.
Yet the quest to satisfy it
is nothing less than magnificent.

The Sound of Love

You know he is "The One"
when you know of yourself...

True Love speaks loudest to the heart in silence.

The Flame of Love

You know he is "The One"
when you know of yourself...

that you are his soul mate

and

two souls that are bound together through time

will always find their way back home.

The Recognition of Love

You know he is "The One"
when you know of yourself...

You are "The One."

About the Author

"Today is the day!" This Mantra holds my life together. As I look back in retrospect, I can say of myself, that I am a consummate dreamer.

I believe beyond a glimmer of doubt that dreams will come true. I can say of myself that I always see the glass half-filled. Perspective is everything, if you are to succeed. So many times, I have failed to accomplish what I have set out to do.

So many times, I have said, "Never again."

It is true what one declares about never...
as soon as you say "never"
you do the one thing you vowed you would not do!

Now, I only say "never" when I am certain I will do a thing again. It is my personal cosmic joke.

I love people. I have so much fun discovering what makes them tick. People bring me the greatest joy.

My greatest belief is that true love exists, as some of y'all have probably gathered from "Rise!"

True love comes to you when you least expect it!

Remember that always.

I grew up in the Mt. Airy section of Philadelphia. I have two younger brothers, Lenny and Tink, both really kewl. Growing up was awesome in Mt. Airy. We were deprived of nothing. Although our parents worked hard and saved every penny to make ends meet, they gave us just about anything we wanted. I had a wonderful home and childhood to the credit of my parents.

I made friends growing up, but I never really fit in. I was always on the outskirts of this group or that group, before being accepted.

In hind-sight, this "singling out by my peers," oftentimes mean-spirited, gave me the strength that would later become invaluable.

In business, I will stand up to anyone for the good of a cause. In my personal life, I am okay with being alone. I spend most of my time... writing. I am contented in my own space. Strength equals resilience.

Women have been through it all. Cast or creed exempted few. I will share my favorite movie list with you later. It will change your life. I could give you a list of books to read, however, you probably would not read them.

My favorite poet is Lord Byron. I had the privilege of sitting in his grotto on the rock- strewn cliff of Portovenere, Italy, a few months ago. You can still feel his energy.

The sea is so rough and forceful there. It refuses to be ignored. Personally, I could never write there. I would only write melancholy drama. Perhaps in his day, the sea spoke to him differently.

The Age of Enlightenment is my favorite period in History. Do yourself a favor. Go to the library and discover the contributions the great thinkers of this era gave to mankind. It spans medicine, religion, science, politics, astronomy, and society. It is most incredible. Voltaire, Rousseau and Benjamin Franklin opened the door to "Free Thought" and paved the way to who we are today.

Travel runs through my veins. At the end of my senior year of High School, I went to Spain. It was awesome and I was hooked. Europe is my natural home. The people are so kind. There is no pretense.

Okay, maybe I am jaded a bit because I work in Hollywood, but come on. It is so nice to go to dinner with people that are genuinely concerned with the "Plight of the Balkans," rather than asking you the superficial question, "So... What do you do?

I hate that. As soon as I hear that, I am out of there. Why do people size you up before they can accept you? I usually say, "I don't do anything, I am finding myself." That clears the room rather quickly.

Back on the trail. I moved to Los Angeles to pursue an acting career. I was successful in landing small roles in film and television, but a cold hard reality suddenly hit me in the face. I was never gonna get the roles I wanted.

In short, I wasn't blonde. I disliked playing the demeaning roles that they offered sisters at the time.

So, I flipped the script. I changed up my game plan and went behind the scenes. This was "The Show." That is where the real power is anyway. Finally, I found a place for myself where I could excel. Artist management is so easy for me. Being a good listener, identifying the needs of the client, and on time delivery, gets them paid. How hard is that?

This was clearly the place I could use my "People skills and win." I love making money of my own. It is a wonderful feeling.

As time went by, I became restless. The financial security was nice but I wasn't growing. I wasn't fulfilling any of my dreams. I watched everyone else soar to the top, by my hands. Yet, I was like a little child with his nose pressed up to the glass window of a candy store.

I could see my dreams.
They were within reach,
but they were always on the other side of the glass.

Boredom breeds discontent, so I had to find a way to lift myself up and salvage my soul. I began to write. I have written four screen-plays to date. Okay so, it was naïve of me to think that I could get my films financed. Thank God, I hadn't thought about that before I began to write. I probably would have never finished any of the scripts.

Writing is my way of escaping to "Worlds beyond my reach." I get to live and love through the characters I create. My most treasured work is entitled, "The Intent of Breeding." I dedicate it to Jane Austin.

It is the story of a dying Prince whose dream is to unite the principalities of Italy into one nation. In the 18th century, Italy was comprised of city-states. It wasn't until Garibaldi, 100 years later, that Italy became nationalized. I wrote this piece in Victorian prose. It is set in the year 1755, Italy.

Someday I will have it published just for the read. It is very special. The rest of the films are, well, uhh, Interesting! I get the "A" for effort but it really stands for "Well Allrighty then!"

When you are lonely, write.
When you are unhappy, write.
When you are in love, write.
Writing is great medicine.

My return to Spain was spectacular. I actually went to visit a friend on holiday a few summers ago. Barcelona is "Off the Hook." The nightlife is unparalleled. The music is hypnotic.

I love to dance. House music is my thang, not techno. I can dance all night if the music is good. That is how I got in hot water in Spain. Okay here goes, my friend, went to the bar to get some drinks for us and left me on the dance floor. So, I kept on dancing alone. I don't know where the Water Polo team came from, but the next thing I knew, I was dancin' on a table in the center of a "Sea of Hotteez." I wasn't mad, but my friend, was steaming. Latin blood runs hot. Anyway, I stayed in Spain as long as I thought it was politically correct. Don't worry, we are still friends.

Next stop, Paris. The first time I saw the Arc d'Triumph and the Champs Elysee, I went crazy. I knew I had to stay. So I did. I rented a flat and walked to the Louvre everyday.

It was in Paris that I discovered my love of classical music. My girl-friend had a little piano in her flat and asked me to play some-thing. I didn't know how.

We had been drinking a fabulous french red wine, so I started to make up a song. It was so beautiful. We couldn't believe it. We thought the wine sweetened the melody so we taped it on her answering machine, just in case. That is how I began to compose. I will compose all of the music for my "Talk Show."

Jamaica has given me such a powerful understanding of life, love and Rastafari. The first time I went there, I was on a Reggae tour with a client.

It was the first time I really became acquainted with the life of Bob Marley and his immense contributions to humanity. I began to study everything I could regarding Haile Selassie I, Solomon and Sheba.

My greatest education has been given to me through travel. The road to Italy has unveiled for me the destiny I have my whole life been in search of. I will move there one day for sure. There are no words to describe Rome, Venice and Subiaco.

I have felt closest to God in the monastery of San Benedetto in Subiaco. The peace and serenity is sublime. The fountains of Rome are breath taking. The shoes in San Marco… girlfriend, please. Yes, Venice is overflowing with Masterworks and timeless architectural treasures. The Square at San Marco, in its own right is magnificent. But the shoes…

Sicily at Christmas is also priceless. My favorite town is Scicli. It is a neighboring town just outside of Pozzallo. I only spent a few days in Amsterdam, Cologne, and London on business, but I will go back some day.

My initial exposure to the New Age world arose when I represented a well-known flamenco guitarist.

The "label makers couldn't be creative enough" to allow it to fall into the category of, to put it simply, good music. So, I would go to the Whole Life Expo and other conventions with my artist. I would always find something missing in the seminars and lectures.

The speakers were credible but they were not real. There was an entire section of "us" that had no voice, no one to turn to and no where to go for advice. I define "us" as those that do not fit into any box.

My first book, Infinite Resolution, opened the door for me to fill this void on the New Age bookstore circuit.

Although I was unpublished, I gave good lecture and there was always a Star or two in the audience.

LA is so predictible, but I was off to a great start. My private celebrity clientele became incredibly profitable and I was always overbooked, even though I was not a PHD.

I still wanted more. I wanted to reach out and touch those that had no where to go. Those that were like me... Always on the outside looking in.

This work... "Rise! The Tao of the Diva" is what I have chosen to do with my life. I am sure there are many of you out there that are discontent with "Having your nose pressed up against the glass window of a candy store." It is not a good feeling. Although I have been fortunate and I have had many successes in my life, none of them belonged to me.

Today is the day... means to me, all that you have waited for, all that you have struggled and sacrificed for, all that you have dreamed of, and all that you deserve will come to you.

When you wake up and proclaim to the universe that
"Today is the day"...
One day it will be!

My Tapestry... mia dolce vita

A monument to timeless memories

For I have seen beyond the horizon

and

pierced the blue of sky

I float among the "Bliss-filled" stars

and sip the elixir of anticipation

For tomorrow holds for me a long awaited treasure

My soul cries out with joy to come

This is the ecstasy that nourishes me

For I have found greatness among my friends.

RISE! The TAO of The DIVA
is dedicated to

To Christiana Noelle Hooks also known as Little Star...
Loving you is my greatest blessing.
You have taught me well and I absolutely adore you.

To Larry, Marjorie and the Guess family
Tink, Sharon, Jasmine, and Jamilla Guess... Nice!
James Brown, James Fitts, Russell Green, Lunette Guess
and
Eloise Green
Your contribution to my life is immeasurable.

To my colleagues, friends and those that inspire me...

Klaus Hallig
You are a dream weaver, Thank You for "Rising" above Hollywood
and standing for what is good and right at the core of every heart

Reverend Michael Beckwith
You are the Sun... the Way Shower, lighting the way

Stephen J. Cannell
Your writing inspires me like the noble cause of Arthur
The legend precedes you

Tom Ford
Your artistry defines my sensibility...
and all that I feel when I am beautiful.

Alberto Ferrari
Your hospitality and generosity is fathomless

Vanetia Fluellen
You put the "D" in Diva
You knew we'd see this day

Davide Falkner and Sasa Crnogorac
You are Fabu

Lawrence Hilton-Jacobs
True friendship is a rare gift

Bertha Joffrion
Make the most of each day
Something good is bound to happen

Broderick Johnson and Andrew Cosove
There are no words to express
How immensely proud I am to know you both.

George Lucas
I sat in your chair and knew that the force was with me
and then you walked into the room ...
and I felt that maybe I too would, "Rise!"
I would like to eat what you eat for breakfast.

Patrick LeLoup
Success belongs to those who claim it
It's your turn!

Maxi Priest
You introduced me to Jah
Be ever wonderful

Karen Rae
When no one else believed...
You were there

Shanna Rosen
You are charming, beautiful and incredibly talented
Don't stop til' you get enough

Gianluca Rossato
Tu sai sempre vicino...

Barry Satchwell
Follow the voice within your heart
embrace the call

Antonio Sabato Jr.
The saga of Batman Lives on!
See you at the top

Christian Sottana
The Lion of San Marco stands at the threshold of destiny
You are the future of Venice

Lolly and Tony Stark
This is just the beginning...
I am so thrilled to have you in my life

Pete Steinberg
I will always remember your kindness

Micah Theard
No matter where I go... you will always be there

Adrienne Thomas
You are so flawless...
The ultimate Diva

Deddy Tzur
Your music is the voice of your soul
It is a privilege to listen

Uncle Woody
Q Psi, without you the world of music would miss a beat

Phil Wurtzel
The journey to Falkirk is a great adventure, Bona Fortuna

LeLe Zanette, Tommy Mezzavilla, Marcello Canzian,
Luca and Amici di Prosecco
Venice is unforgettable
So are all of you

To my posse... gratitude and affection

Attila, Jason, Chris, Michael, Todd, Bill, Pierluigi, Stefano, P.J., Paola
and Carlo, Mirko, Toma, Alfredo, Guiseppe, Lele, Ray, Ivan, Deb,
Gail, Sung, Minoo, Luigi, Clay, Michi, Roz, Gabby, Mel, Kerline, Art,
Brett, Nikki, Armin, Anouar, David, John, Sylvia, Flore, Giamba, Isaaco,
Kelly, and Matt.

Special Thanks

David Brenner
Rocio Briceno
Kathryn Bishop
Thomas Carter
Jacob Caracappa
Henry Castellanos
Todd Colllins
Bill Frank
Dr. Ivan Gulas
Clint Greenleaf
Kim Jakwerth
Brian Loucks
Steveland Morris
Fred Mouawad
Pat O'Brien
Nathan and Yvonne Oliver
Jorge Penos
Lance Powell
Lionel Ritchie
Mark Stendhal
Quentin Tarantino
Paul Wiley
Billy Zane
Moon Zappa

To The City of Philadelphia
There is no place like home
Thank You

Senator Vincent Fumo
Jonathan Saidel
The Honorable James De Leon
Larry Guess Jr.
James Harrity
Dr. Gregory Nelson
Doug Henderson
Charles Highsmith
Don Yun
Jackie Fulton - Benain
Butterball
Dr. Anthony Farrow
Donita Nero
Don Pak
Ed Hanlon

My Favorite Filmz

My Favorite Filmz

Swept from the Sea
Boy meets girl and they fall in love against all odds.
Vincent Perez is so sexy, he shines.

Wilde
Boy meets boy and they fall in love against all odds.
Jude Law is breathtaking in the telling of the life of Oscar Wilde.

Angels and Insects
Boy meets girl and falls in love but girl has dark secret.
Phillip Haas is a master director.

Cousin Bette
Revenge is sweet.
Never underestimate the wrath of a scorned woman.
This is Jessica Lang's best performance.

How Green was my Valley
Love conquers all.
The most powerful force in the world is the family
Child star, Roddy Mc Dowell is wonderful.

Ridicule
Wit reigned and decadence ruled while the peasants starved to
death. A visual masterpiece.

Tea with Mussolini
The Diva brigade give the nazis a run for their money.
Cher rules.

Solomon and Gaenor
Jewish boy meets Welsh girl and they fall in love against all odds.
Ioan Gruffudd is a major Hottee.
He also portrays Horatio Hornblower on A and E.

Middle March
Love, fortunes, and aristocracy weave a web
of deceit and intrigue. Rufus Sewell ... ooh La La.

Mansfield Park
Protocol shapes the face of love and honor.
Jonny Lee Miller is so damn fine.

Her Majesty Mrs. Brown
Behind every Royal Diva stands a real man.
Dame Judy is the best actress in the entire universe.

Horseman on the Roof
Plague and war ravish France.
Damsel in distress falls in love with Italian officer.
Olivier Martinez is dripping sensuality. He is every girlz dream guy.

Where Angels Fear to Tread
Treachery, deceit, murder, and love... This is a "Must See."
Rupert Graves is one of my favorite actors.
Of course, he's a hottee too.

The Buccaneers
Debutantes go abroad in search of titled husbands during the London season. James Frain is stellar as the Duke. This is a cast of hotteez.

Fiorile
Karmic evolution is the center of this story
of three generations of an Italian family.

Persuasion
Miss Jane Austin is working her magic.
When Jane is in the house, no writer shines brighter.

Farinelli
This is the saga of the life and loves of an Italian Castrato.
Stefano Dianesi is spectacular as Farinelli.

La Strada
Fellini doing his thang.

Wide Sargasso Sea
The seductive counterpart to Jane Eyre.

Great Expectations

A young boy finds his way into society by the hand of an unknown benefactor. Ioan Gruffudd stars in the jewel of Dickens. I adore him.

Wagner

The great composer finds a true friend and financier in the king of Bavaria, Ludwig II.

The Irish RM

A whimsical, warm and witty look at life in the Irish countryside, Ireland is the star of this piece, the culture and its people.

Sense and Sensibility

My girl, Jane, giving it to you like no other,
Hugh Grant is so fabu.

An Ideal Husband

A perpetual bachelor must finally settle down and marry.
Rupert Everett is gorgeous and quite brilliant.

Up at the Villa

A one night stand ends in murder and concealment during Mussolini's reign. Sean Penn works my nerves and gives you fever. Directed by Phillip Haas, my favorite auteur.

Orlando

The magical reincarnations of an aristocrat as he changes from male to female. Tilda Swinton plays both sexes with the ease of a magician.

King and I

A wonderful tale of the life of the King of Siam,
Yul brenner is the number 1 "old school" Hottee.
Check him out. He is dazzling.

Butterflies are Free

Blind boy meets girl and opens her eyes to true love. Eddie Albert Jr. is a show stopper and should have been a superstar based on this performance.

Notting Hill

She loves me... she loves me not, boy meets girl, they marry, Oh my Goodness... This is Hugh Grant at his finest.
Where can I get one of those?

Only You

Girl searches for her true love in Italy after a bout of cold feet. Honey, Robert Downey Jr. is soooooooooo amazing. Billy Zane sizzles.

Brideshead Revisted
A dazzling anthology of the life and times of British aristocracy.
Jeremy Irons is sensuous and masterful in this British series.

Dying Young
Love can conquer all. A dying man falls in love with his nurse.
Campbell Scott is a major Hottee.
He is warm, sensitive, strong, sexy, and gorgeous.

Shakespeare in Love
A romantic telling of the life of the famous penman,
Joseph Fiennes is "Off the Hook."

Basil
Boy meets girl, falls in love and gets swindled out of his inheritance.
Jared Leto is a Babe.

Most of these filmz are available at your local videostore.

Enjoy!

To Order
Rise! The Tao of the Diva

Please detach or photocopy this form

$14.95

Please include $3.00 for shipping and handling per book within the United States or $4.00 per book for international shipping and handling. For UPS 2nd day delivery add $10.00 per book (available in the United States only) California residents please add 7.5% sales tax.

_____

Please make check or money order payable to: Michelangelo Publishing

Mail to:
Michelangelo Publishing
8491 West Sunset Blvd. #160
Los Angeles, Ca, 90069

I would like to order _____ copies at $14.95 each   = _____

Shipping USA _____ books at $3.00 each   = _____

Shipping International _____ books at $4.00 each   = _____

Shipping UPS 2nd Day _____ books at $10.00 each   = _____

Subtotal   = _____

7.5% sales tax (Ca. Residents only)   = _____

Total Enclosed   = _____

Ship To:

Name _____

Address _____

City _____ State _____ Zip _____

Country_____ Telephone _____

E mail address: _____

If this is a gift, please add "From"_____

To Order
Rise! The Tao of the Diva

Please detach or photocopy this form

$14.95

Please include $3.00 for shipping and handling per book within the United States or $4.00 per book for international shipping and handling. For UPS 2nd day delivery add $10.00 per book (available in the United States only) California residents please add 7.5% sales tax.

_____

Please make check or money order payable to: Michelangelo Publishing

Mail to:
Michelangelo Publishing
8491 West Sunset Blvd. #160
Los Angeles, Ca, 90069

I would like to order _____ copies at $14.95 each   = _____

Shipping USA _____ books at $3.00 each   = _____

Shipping International _____ books at $4.00 each   = _____

Shipping UPS 2nd Day _____ books at $10.00 each   = _____

Subtotal   = _____

7.5% sales tax (Ca. Residents only)   = _____

Total Enclosed   = _____

Ship To:
Name _____
Address _____
City _____ State _____ Zip _____
Country_____ Telephone _____
E mail address: _____
If this is a gift, please add "From"_____

To Order
Rise! The Tao of the Diva

Please detach or photocopy this form

$14.95

Please include $3.00 for shipping and handling per book within the United States or $4.00 per book for international shipping and handling. For UPS 2nd day delivery add $10.00 per book (available in the United States only) California residents please add 7.5% sales tax.

Please make check or money order payable to: Michelangelo Publishing

Mail to:
Michelangelo Publishing
8491 West Sunset Blvd. #160
Los Angeles, Ca, 90069

I would like to order _____ copies at $14.95 each = _____

Shipping USA _____ books at $3.00 each = _____

Shipping International _____ books at $4.00 each = _____

Shipping UPS 2nd Day _____ books at $10.00 each = _____

Subtotal = _____

7.5% sales tax (Ca. Residents only) = _____

Total Enclosed = _____

Ship To:

Name _____

Address _____

City _____ State _____ Zip _____

Country_____ Telephone _____

E mail address: _____

If this is a gift, please add "From"_____

To Order
Rise! The Tao of the Diva

Please detach or photocopy this form

$14.95

Please include $3.00 for shipping and handling per book within the United States or $4.00 per book for international shipping and handling. For UPS 2nd day delivery add $10.00 per book (available in the United States only) California residents please add 7.5% sales tax.

_____

Please make check or money order payable to: Michelangelo Publishing

Mail to:
Michelangelo Publishing
8491 West Sunset Blvd. #160
Los Angeles, Ca, 90069

I would like to order _____ copies at $14.95 each   = _____

Shipping USA _____ books at $3.00 each   = _____

Shipping International _____ books at $4.00 each   = _____

Shipping UPS 2nd Day _____ books at $10.00 each   = _____

Subtotal   = _____

7.5% sales tax (Ca. Residents only)   = _____

Total Enclosed   = _____

Ship To:

Name _____

Address _____

City _____ State _____ Zip _____

Country_____ Telephone _____

E mail address: _____

If this is a gift, please add "From"_____

To Order
Rise! The Tao of the Diva

Please detach or photocopy this form

$14.95

Please include $3.00 for shipping and handling per book within the United States or $4.00 per book for international shipping and handling. For UPS 2nd day delivery add $10.00 per book (available in the United States only) California residents please add 7.5% sales tax.

Please make check or money order payable to: Michelangelo Publishing

Mail to:
Michelangelo Publishing
8491 West Sunset Blvd. #160
Los Angeles, Ca, 90069

I would like to order _____ copies at $14.95 each   = _____

Shipping USA _____ books at $3.00 each   = _____

Shipping International _____ books at $4.00 each   = _____

Shipping UPS 2nd Day _____ books at $10.00 each   = _____

Subtotal   = _____

7.5% sales tax (Ca. Residents only)   = _____

Total Enclosed   = _____

Ship To:

Name _____

Address _____

City _____ State _____ Zip _____

Country_____ Telephone _____

E mail address: _____

If this is a gift, please add "From" _____

Notes

Notes

Notes

Notes

Notes